What Are My Chances?

by Margie Burton, Cathy French, and Tammy Jones

Table of Contents

Which One Will I Choose?

Today, I opened my sock drawer and looked inside. I saw three pairs of socks.

There were two white pairs. There was one red pair.

I closed my eyes and pulled one pair
out of the drawer.

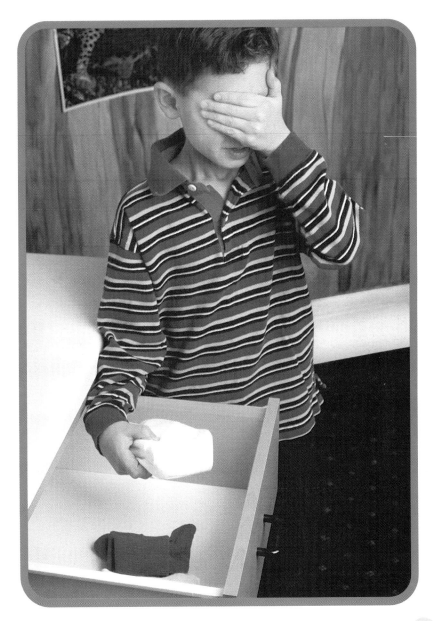

I wanted to pick the pair of red socks,
but I picked a pair of white socks.
So, I got dressed and put on the white socks.

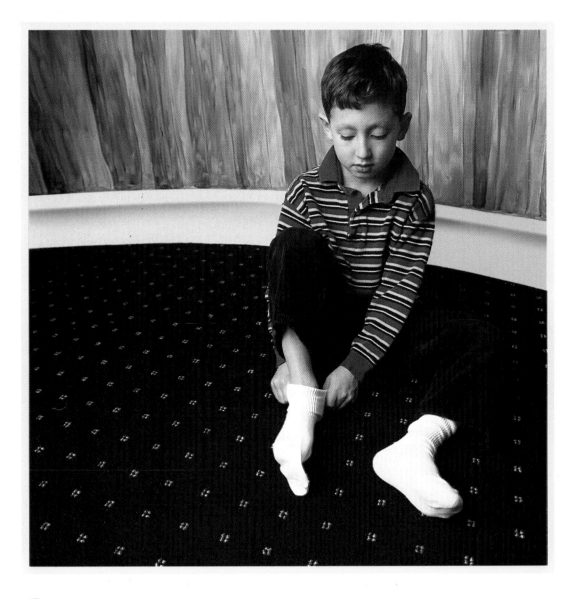

For breakfast I wanted a chocolate donut. My sister wanted a chocolate one, too. There was only one chocolate donut left. The other three had sprinkles.

My mom told me to close my eyes and pick one.

I wanted to pick the chocolate donut,
but I picked a sprinkled one.
So, I ate the sprinkled donut,
and then went to school.

What Will I Get?

When it was time for snacks at school, my teacher gave out apples and oranges. She gave apples to some children and oranges to others.

When it was my turn, she had an apple in one hand and an orange in the other. I wanted an apple.

I thought that I would get the orange, but I got the apple this time.

I told my teacher that I was so happy.
I told her about the times before when
I had not gotten what I wanted.
This time I did.

My teacher said that it would have been hard for me to get what I wanted all the time. If there are more white socks than red socks, then the chances are good that I will pick white socks.

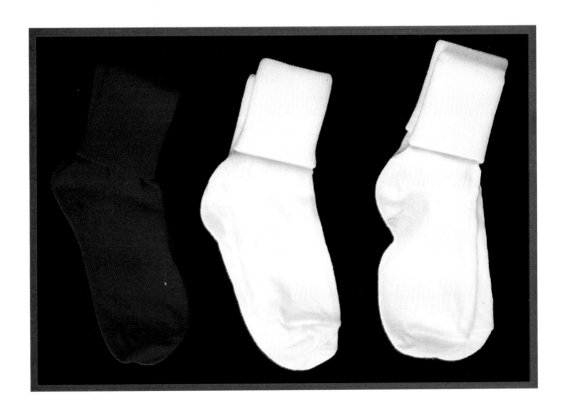

If there are more sprinkled donuts than chocolate donuts, then the chances are good that I will pick sprinkled donuts.

If there are the same number of apples and oranges, then I have as good a chance of getting an apple as I do of getting an orange.

Will I Get Heads or Tails?

My teacher said that each time you toss a coin,
you have just as good a chance of getting heads
as you do of getting tails.

heads   tails

She also told me that if you toss the coin
over and over, you have a good chance
of getting the same number of heads as tails.

She gave each of us a coin and told us
to toss it four times.

We made a chart to show what happened.

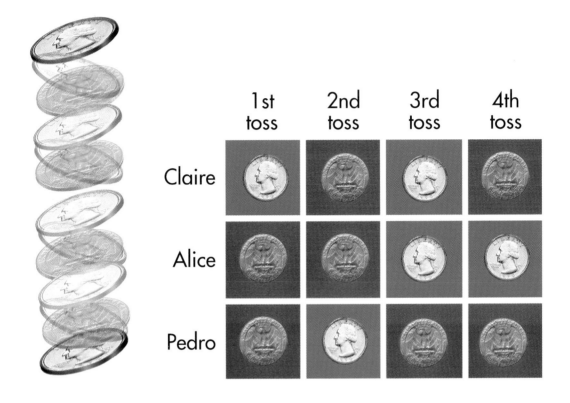

	1st toss	2nd toss	3rd toss	4th toss
Claire				
Alice				
Pedro				

What would you get if you tossed a coin
with your friends at school?